I0164161

THE GRACE OF GOD

REVEALED

IN THE DEATH OF MAN

BY KARL CRAWFORD

Most of us fear death and cling to life. Death, unless Jesus Christ returns to take up His people before they die, is inevitable for all of us. The Word of God says, *"It is appointed unto men once to die, but after this the judgment"* (Hebrews 9:27). But God is able to take the *"sting of death"* and turn it to victory and redeem even this dreaded event in our life.

All Scriptures from the King James Version

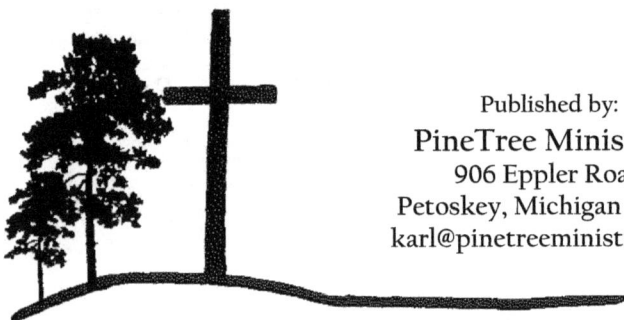

Published by:
PineTree Ministries
906 Eppler Road
Petoskey, Michigan 49770
karl@pinetreeministries.org

COPYRIGHT @ 2012 BY KARL CRAWFORD, PETOSKEY, MICHIGAN.
ALL RIGHTS RESERVED

Introduction

It is common with most of us to have an aversion to death. Someone was asked what it was he would like to be remembered for and we sympathize with his answer. He replied "I would like to be remembered as being the oldest man who ever lived." He would have to go some to beat Methuselah's 969 years but he was willing to do his part.

One of the curses for Adam and Eve's sin was physical death and to us it is still a curse. We question the mental state of those who talk about death too much and we are sad for those whose loss of hope causes them to commit suicide. Others refuse to talk about death at all, believing that if they ignore it that somehow it may not come to them.

My mother was a vigorous woman. She lived that way and she wanted to leave this world the same way. Probably her greatest fear was being an invalid. She did not want to be in a long-term care home and have other people care for her. When she was in her 70s and early 80s, she would ask anyone who would listen, "Who would ever want to live to be 90?" I would try to reassure her that there were indeed some 90 year old people who were vibrant, healthy and still doing the work of the Lord but to no avail. One day I found the answer to her question in the Reader's Digest. The answer to who would ever want to be 90 is, "Anyone who is 89." It is normal for us to hold to this life, even when life is hard, and even when we are 89.

The Apostle Paul stated his view of death in the book of Philippians *"For to me to live is Christ, and to die is gain. But if I live in the flesh, this is the fruit of my labour: yet what I shall choose I wot not. For I am in a strait betwixt two, having a desire to depart, and to be with Christ; which is far better: Nevertheless to abide in the flesh is more needful for you."*[1] Paul was torn between a life of Christ's ministry here or life with Christ there which is *"far better."*

We hold to life and avoid thinking of death. It is hard for us to believe that God, in His grace, can redeem even death. What men fear and fight against is precious in His sight. What we view as separation from life and Loved ones He sees as our joining Him, our dearest loved One, in a far better place. The vapor of life we hold to so dearly, He replaces with eternal life with Him. The unknown becomes the most fully known.[2]

---

1 Philippians 1:21-24

2 1 Corinthians 13:12 *For now we see through a glass, darkly; but then face to face: now I know in part; but then shall I know even as also I am known.*

A Long Walk

'Abraham. Take your son Isaac to the mountain and sacrifice his life to Me.'[3] Can you imagine hearing those words and then beginning the three day journey to Mt. Moriah with your son? Abraham believed that he indeed was doomed to take his own son's life. He believed that God would raise Isaac from the dead, but it would be his hand, holding the knife he had been careful to pack for the trip that would take the life from the son God had promised Sarah and him. Can you imagine Sarah waiting at home? Did she believe that God would raise Isaac from the dead, or was she fearful that Abraham would come back alone? Not only was it a three day journey to the mountain, but it was a three day journey back from the mountain. No cell phone or texting would carry the news to Sarah that God had provided a lamb. There would be another three day journey for Abraham and Isaac to carry the wondrous news home.

Moses took a long walk as well, his coming at the end of his fascinating life. In Deuteronomy 32:48-52, God told Moses to go up to the top of Mount Nebo...to

---

3 Genesis 22:1-2. And it came to pass after these things, that God did tempt Abraham, and said unto him, Abraham: and he said, Behold, here I am. And he said, Take now thy son, thine only son Isaac, whom thou lovest, and get thee into the land of Moriah; and offer him there for a burnt offering upon one of the mountains which I will tell thee of.

die. His journey was much shorter than Abraham's. Mt. Nebo is 2,620 feet in height and Moses probably walked no further than a couple of miles depending on how far the Israelite camp was from the base of the mountain.[4] He was 120 years old at the time but, according to the Scriptures, in extremely good health. He was not feeble by man's standards and could have lived many more years. However, God came to him in this passage and reminded him of the sentence of death. The verdict of death had seemed afar off previously, but now Moses was confronted with its immediacy.

> *And the LORD spake unto Moses that selfsame day, saying, Get thee up into this mountain Abarim, unto mount Nebo, which is in the land of Moab, that is over against Jericho; and behold the land of Canaan, which I give unto the children of Israel for a possession: And die in the mount whither thou goest up, and be gathered unto thy people; as Aaron thy brother died in mount Hor, and was gathered unto his people: Because ye trespassed against me among the children of Israel at the waters of Meribah-Kadesh, in the wilderness of Zin; because ye sanctified me not in the midst of the children of Israel. Yet thou shalt see the land before thee; but thou shalt not go thither unto the land which I give the children of Israel.*
> *Deuteronomy 32:48-52*

Moses had met God before and in very unique ways. He met Him at the burning bush, and he met Him at Mt. Sinai for the giving and receiving of the law. God met Moses in the cleft of the rock, where Moses caught a glimpse of God Himself. Moses' face

---

4 Many scholars believe the people in the camp could see Moses on the top of the mountain. If this is true, the distance certainly could not be great.

Moses had prayed that God would relent and allow him to go into the Promised Land.

I pray thee, let me go over, and see the good land that is beyond Jordan, that goodly mountain, and Lebanon. But the Lord was wroth with me for your sakes, and would not hear me: and the Lord said unto me, Let it suffice thee; speak no more unto me of this matter.

Deuteronomy 3:25-26

God had told him to "speak no more" of it and there is no record in Scripture that Moses ever prayed about this again.

shown with the glory of God after spending time in His presence. Now Moses would meet God in another unique way. The meeting took place on Mt. Nebo, also called Mt. Pisgah, as he, literally, 'met his Maker.'

Before he began this last journey, Moses blessed the people. He named each of the tribes and pronounced God's blessing upon them. He began to close the blessing with one of my favorite passages in all of God's Word, *"There is none like unto the God of Jeshurun,[5] who rideth upon the heaven in thy help, and in his excellency on the sky. The eternal God is thy refuge, and underneath are the everlasting arms:"* (Deuteronomy 33:26-27a). Moses spoke these great words about the God who had just reminded him of the sentence of death, a sentence pronounced on him a year earlier when he had struck the rock and dishonored God. It is important to note that there is no sign of bitterness in Moses. There is not a hint of Asaph's words in Psalm 73 *"Surely God is good to Israel, but as for me..."*

---

5 Jeshurun means "the anointed one" signifying the people of God. This is a new name given to the people as they prepared to cross the Jordan into the Promised Land.

Deuteronomy 7 is such a beautiful passage of God's Word. Here He reminds His people that He did not choose them because they were the greatest of nations but because they were the least of the nations. He chose them to Himself to be a holy people—His people.

The New Testament teaches the exact same principle.

For ye see your calling, brethren, how that not many wise men after the flesh, not many mighty, not many noble, are called: But God hath chosen the foolish things of the world to confound the wise; and God hath chosen the weak things of the world to confound the things which are mighty; And base things of the world, and things which are despised, hath God chosen, yea, and things which are not, to bring to nought things that are: That no flesh should glory in his presence.

1 Corinthians 1:26-29

Both passages remind us of the privilege of being chosen by God—a gift not given because of who we are but because of who He is.

I have to wonder what would be going through my mind at this time if I were Moses. Being the leader of the Israelites for 40 years, he knew many of these people who would be going into the Promised Land. Maybe he knew that Achan had a penchant for pretty things, and that his character was that of a disobedient thief. Maybe he knew of character flaws in a number of the people that stood before him that day, the ones he was now pronouncing God's blessing on; the ones who would be crossing into the Promised Land while he stayed behind on Mt. Pisgah's heights. He certainly knew they were a fickle, rebellious people. He had experienced that for the past 40 years. But there is no hint that he was disappointed with God; there is no pleading with God to reconsider His verdict of death. Hear his words, *"Happy art thou, O Israel: who is like unto thee, O people saved by the Lord, the Shield of thy help, and who is the Sword of thy excellency!"* Deuteronomy 33:29.

It is said that a person's words just before their pending death are perhaps the most important they will ever speak. They are words that show their heart, their passion, their hopes and their fears. They are not wasted words, because the dying one knows this is their last opportunity to speak. Moses' last words were to remind God's people of the sufficiency of God and of His desire to bless them.

When Aaron was about to die, he and his son, Eleazer, and Moses went up to Mt. Hor together. When Moses was to die he began the walk towards the mountain—alone. God had told him he would see the land, but He did not tell him that He would meet him at the mountain's summit. What must have been going through his mind? He made the climb to the top of the mountain because his *"natural force"* was still strong. And he met God there.

For a man who was about to face death at the hand of his Judge, this was an extremely intimate meeting. *"And the Lord shewed"*[6] Moses the land, the Promised Land that God's people had been looking forward to inhabiting since the promise was first made to Abraham—a land flowing with milk and honey. It was a beautiful, fertile land for a small nation. The

---

6 Deuteronomy 34:1-3 *And Moses went up from the plains of Moab unto the mountain of Nebo, to the top of Pisgah, that is over against Jericho. And the Lord shewed him all the land of Gilead, unto Dan, And all Naphtali, and the land of Ephraim, and Manasseh, and all the land of Judah, unto the utmost sea, And the south, and the plain of the valley of Jericho, the city of palm trees, unto Zoar.*

nation could never have had this land on its own. The Israelites inherited it because God had set His affections on them (Deuteronomy 7:6-10).

God pointed out to Moses the land that the people would inherit and showed him where the various tribes would be located. It must have been a thrilling time for Moses to catch the first glimpse of the Land and to have the Lord Himself as his guide. After all, he had spent the last 40 years of his life leading and walking with these people to the Jordan. But as intimate as this meeting was, the Judge's verdict was not lifted, and the appointed time came.

Some see the events leading up to this final scene as those of a vindictive God who lost His temper when Moses struck the rock. Moses had spent almost 120 years of devotion to God. He had spent his last 40 years as one of the Nation's greatest prophets. Yet God refused him entrance into the Promised Land! Where was grace? Where was forgiveness? Where was the God of second, and third chances? God seems to have forgiven far greater sins than this for other men. Where was fairness? Where was justice?

Some say Moses could not go into the Land because he struck the rock instead of speaking to it, as the Lord had instructed. Some say it was because he struck the rock twice. Some say it was because he struck it in anger. Others say it was because Moses said *"have not WE* (implying God and I or implying he and Aaron) *provided for you?"* in one way putting himself on an equal footing with God and in the other implying that he and Aaron had provided the water without God's help.

Some say that Moses, as the giver of the law, could not enter into the Promised Land because that role was reserved for Joshua, the picture or type of Jesus

Christ. They believe if Moses had not struck the rock, he would have committed some other sin that would have caused God to ban him entry.

I hold to the latter view, believing that Moses could not go into the Promised Land because his death was a picture of law and grace. God took Moses, the lawgiver, to the mountain to show him what his leadership had accomplished. However, the 'law' could go no further. Paul calls the law a schoolmaster,[7] which taught us the lessons that grace would fulfill. Moses' death just short of the Promised Land and Joshua's leading the people across the Jordan into the land is a glimpse of Christ's fulfillment of the requirements of the Law.

While we may disagree about the reason Moses could not go into the land we plainly see the grace of God shown to Moses in these last few moments of his earthly life. God could have struck Moses dead at the split second his rod struck the rock. After Moses' final blessing upon the people, God could have caused him to keel over dead in front of them, as a sign to them to be careful not only <u>to</u> obey but to be careful <u>how</u> to obey. Instead, God met Moses at the top of the mountain *face to face...as a man speaketh unto his friend* (Exodus 33:11). God could have simply given Moses a vision of the Promised Land before he died, but instead He personally pointed out to him the expanse of the Land. He had not done this for Abraham, Isaac, Jacob, Joseph, or Aaron. This privilege was reserved for Moses alone.

Stepping back from Scripture for a second, I see the scene playing out something like this: God allowed Moses to soak in the beauty of the Land, letting him imagine in his mind's eye the people crossing

7 Galatians 3:24-25 *Wherefore the law was our schoolmaster to bring us unto Christ, that we might be justified by faith. But after that faith is come, we are no longer under a schoolmaster.*

the Jordan and beginning to take the Land as their own. The Lord knew that Moses would be thinking of the final words of blessing he had spoken to the people only a few hours before *"...and thou shalt tread upon their high places"*, depicting them conquering the nations their fathers had been afraid to face a few years earlier. God's next words to Moses were firm but gentle, 'Friend, it is time. You sit here and lean against Me. Today you will walk through the valley of the shadow of death, and I will walk with you. Close your eyes now and hold My hand Moses. It will be okay.' (Jewish tradition teaches that God kissed Moses, taking his spirit into Himself. Many Bible scholars dispute this view, but it is a beautiful picture of an intimate moment.[8] It also reminds us of the creation of man when God breathed life into Adam.)

When Moses, whose *"eyes were undimmed and whose strength was not abated,"* breathed his last breath, the Lord prepared a grave, gently laid the body of Moses in it, and covered it over with His hand. There was no monument to mark the spot. But the Lord knows where the grave is to this day, awaiting the bodily resurrection.

However you look at the scene as described in Deuteronomy, whether you accept what I believe or not, we see a beautiful demonstration of grace—God's grace.

God didn't have to take Moses to the mountain – but He did.

---

8 At the end, God leans down from the heavens and ends Moses' life with a soft, gentle kiss. This is derived from Deuteronomy 34:5, where it is written, *"So Moses, the servant of the Eternal, died there, in the land of Moab, at the command of the Eternal."* The Hebrew reads, al pi Adonai, *"by the mouth of the Eternal."* Hence the legend about God kissing Moses at his moment of death." From www.myjewishlearning.com

He didn't have to show him the Promised Land – but He did.

He didn't have to personally bury him – but He did.

He didn't have to say "there arose not a prophet since in Israel like unto Moses"[9] – but He did.

He didn't have to choose Moses to be one of the Old Testament figures to verify Christ's ministry at the Mount of Transfiguration[10] – but He did.

The Bible never remembers Moses as the 'one who struck the rock' but instead remembers him as the friend of God, the one whom *"the Lord knew face to face."* And that is grace.

The Lord's message to Moses in Numbers 20 that he could not enter the Land was stark. It shocks our sensibilities. If God said those words to Moses, one of the best of us, then what will He say to us in another fit of anger? What if I do something stupid (not an unheard of notion) and anger Him in some way? To this day Bible scholars do not agree on what part of Moses' words or actions angered God. What chance do I have?

The starkness of God's verdict in Numbers 20, however, cannot be separated from the gracious and loving scene on Mt. Nebo in Deuteronomy 33. One has to see God in both chapters. To us, truth and grace or justice and grace are either totally incompatible, being opposite sides of the same coin, or they exist in great tension. To God, they are natural, beautiful,

---

9   Deuteronomy 34:10

10 Moses eventually did make it into the Promised Land at this tremendously important event in Christ's ministry. See Matthew 17:1-13.

equal facets of His character. God stands firm in His justice, even while showing His great grace. Moses accepted God's justice and basked in His great grace—even in the face of death. He had just spoken those great words to the people, *"the Eternal God is your Refuge, and underneath* (even in the face of death) *are the everlasting arms."* It was then time for him to live them.

Joseph's words may have been in Moses' mind as he closed his eyes, thinking back over his life, *"... but God meant it for good."[11]* What a life he had led, from a babe in the bulrushes, to Pharaoh's palace, to the plagues, to the Red Sea, to the desert years, to leading two million people, to Mt. Sinai, to the rock at Meribah, and to the heights of Mt. Pisgah. There had to have been times when he wondered where God was, when he wondered if God was through with him; and when he wondered if leading that rebellious group of people for forty years was an honor or not. But from his vantage point on Mt. Pisgah, he could not miss the hand of God. He could say with the Apostle Paul, *"and we KNOW that ALL things work together for good to them that love God, to them who are the called according to His purpose"* (Romans 8:28, emphasis mine).

Moses knew, as much as any New Testament saint ever has or ever will, that God is truly the God of justice, but He is also the God of everlasting mercy and of grace.

---

11 Genesis 50:20 *But as for you, ye thought evil against me; but God meant it unto good, to bring to pass, as it is this day, to save much people alive.*

A Precious Time

I have been present at the death of some dear family members. They have been very intimate moments. When my dad died, the family members stood around his now lifeless body and quoted Psalm 23. My brother spent the last months of his life in an unresponsive condition. When the end finally came, his wife and his children and my wife and I gathered around his bedside, where we quoted scripture and sang hymns. When my mother died, having spent the last month of her otherwise vigorous 95 years battling the effects of a stroke, there was a healing of some family problems during and after her hospital stay. In each of these deaths, the person dying was in a coma-like state. I am not sure if the other family members in the room felt the intimate presence of the Lord at the time. I do know that I did.

The Word says that *"precious in the sight of the Lord is the death of his saints."*[12] I believe that the Holy Spirit authored these words to give us a glimpse into the way God looks at the death of His children. Moses' death on Mt. Nebo reveals this precious intimacy between God and man at the time of death. It was such a soul-touching scene there on that mountain with the Lord taking special care to show the man Moses what the spirit Moses would know seconds after his last breath was taken. *"What is man that*

---

12 Psalm 116:15 *Precious in the sight of the LORD is the death of his saints.*

Thou art mindful of him," is a question that any man is forced to ask as he begins to grow in the Lord and to see Him more fully. Why would God be *"mindful"* of these last moments in His child's life?

> *When I consider thy heavens, the work of thy fingers, the moon and the stars, which thou hast ordained; What is man, that thou art mindful of him? and the son of man, that thou visitest him?*
> *Psalm 8:3-4*

Being present at the death of a loved one is a deeply personal time. There are many thoughts and emotions that one must work through. Was this person a believer? What was my relationship with them? What will become of me? Who will I become now that this person is gone? What will happen to the family? These and many other questions will flood through one's mind depending on his relationship with the dying person.

God enters into this intimate time in His own way, in a way that is precious to Him. At the death of Stephen, God opened the windows of heaven,[13] revealing to Stephen a vision of the Father and Son. God's appearance at Stephen's death did not keep him from dying. Rather, He gave to Stephen (and to us) a vision of God the Father and God the Son actively, intimately, invested in these last moments of his life. *"What is man"* that God would spend these last few earthly moments with him? Stephen's death was imminent. In a few moments his spirit would be

---

13 Acts 7:55-56 *But he, being full of the Holy Ghost, looked up stedfastly into heaven, and saw the glory of God, and Jesus standing on the right hand of God, And said, Behold, I see the heavens opened, and the Son of man standing on the right hand of God.*

14

free from the body and in the presence of God. Yet the Father made sure that Stephen knew that He and His Son were there with him in a special, *"precious"* way.

Some 40 years before the scene at Mt. Nebo, God had met Moses at another place, this time in a burning bush whose flames were not quenched. Moses was a vastly different man in this first meeting. This once confident, Egyptian-trained man had spent the last 40 years tending his father-in-law's sheep. During those years he had lost his confidence in himself and in God. As the Lord sought to convince Moses that he, with the Lord's help, could lead His people out of Egypt, Moses asked who he should tell the people has sent him. The Lord said, *"I am that I am."*[14] *"I am"* the one that will supply whatever it is you or My people need! He proved the truth of this name time and again: in the plagues; crossing the Red Sea; pouring water from a rock; sending daily manna; giving protection in battle; being present in miracle after miracle; providing whatever was needed at the time.

At this last intimate earthly meeting, Moses met God on the top of the mountain. God was still the *"I Am"* for him. Scripture records that since his sin at Meribah and God's pronouncement that he and Aaron could not enter the Promised Land, Moses had asked God to reverse His verdict. After leading these people for 40 years, Moses longed to go into the Land with them. God would not relent, but in His role as the *"I Am"*, He met Moses on the mountain and personally showed him the expanse of the Promised Land. From the burning bush to Mt. Nebo, God remained the *"I*

---

14 Exodus 3:14 *And God said unto Moses, I Am That I Am: and he said, Thus shalt thou say unto the children of Israel, I Am hath sent me unto you.*

Am" for Moses. In these last moments of his life, when Moses needed a friend, God was there; when he needed a gravedigger, God was there; when he needed someone to place his body in the grave, God was there. It may seem that Moses walked to the mountain alone, but at the time of his death, he was in the presence of God. Jude recorded later that when his body needed protection from Satan,[15] God was still there for him.

The *"I Am"* for Moses and the Nation of Israel is the same God who promises you that He will *"supply all your need according to His riches in glory by Christ Jesus."*[16] When God told Moses that He was the *"I Am"*, He meant it for all time. When He says *"all"* your need to us, He means that as well—for all time. That is plainly evident in the life and the death of Moses. God is faithful to His promises. He is faithful to his servants—even in death.

---

15 Jude 9

16 Philippians 4:19 *But my God shall supply all your need according to his riches in glory by Christ Jesus.*

I Go to Prepare a Place for You

The picture, from Jewish culture, of a bridegroom preparing a place for he and his bride to live and then coming for her to take her with him is a beautiful passage that shows us what Christ is currently doing for His bride, the church. He is preparing a place, and He is coming back[17] one day to take the church away from this life to spend eternity in the new home He has so lovingly prepared.

Maybe we see a glimpse of the Bridegroom coming for individual believers in the stories of Moses and Stephen. At the time of their deaths, God came in a special way to reassure them, a step in the process that almost seems unnecessary,[18] but God views these times as precious. Enoch and Elijah 'walked with God', and He came for them in a uniquely powerful and intimate way. God comes for His child facing death. This time is precious to Him.

---

17 John 14:1-3 *Let not your heart be troubled: ye believe in God, believe also in me. In my Father's house are many mansions: if it were not so, I would have told you. I go to prepare a place for you. And if I go and prepare a place for you, I will come again, and receive you unto myself; that where I am, there ye may be also.*

18 If we believe that we are "absent from the body and present with the Lord" then what difference do these last earthly moments make? Yet God chooses to come to be with His children in a special, intimate, precious way.

I like to think that not only did the Bridegroom come for Moses, Stephen, Enoch, and Elijah, but that He comes for my loved ones that know Him, and someday will come for me in this special way. Even though His children may be in a coma, in pain, or in the throes of Alzheimer's at the time of their death, God still meets them in an intimate way, taking them from this life to the next. The *"I Am"* is ever the Shepherd. His rod and His staff comfort us, as He walks with us through the *"valley of the shadow of death."*[19]

I may hate the fact that dear loved ones have died, and I may especially hate the fact that some of them suffered greatly before their last breath. Yet it gives me comfort to know that the *"I Am,"* the Good Shepherd of Psalm 23, walked with them in a special way in their passage from this life to the next...just as He promised He would.

---

19 Psalm 23:4 *Yea, though I walk through the valley of the shadow of death, I will fear no evil: for thou art with me; thy rod and thy staff they comfort me.*

For Those Who are not Saints

It is my hope that the previous chapters have provided comfort to God's children, both the ones who are facing their own death and those who have experienced the death of a loved one. However, none of what has been written prior to this offers any comfort to the person who does not know Jesus Christ as his personal Savior. One of the Scriptures used was Psalm 116:15 *"Precious in the sight of the Lord is the death of His saints."* The *"saints"* are the children of God who have accepted His work on the cross as payment for their sins.

Genesis, the first book of the Bible, records the story of Adam and Eve. God had created the heavens and the earth, separated darkness from light, and created the animals, birds, and fishes. He then created Adam in His own image out of the newly formed dust of the ground and breathed His life into Adam. God placed him in the Garden of Eden, telling Adam of the one tree in the entire garden that he could not eat of—the tree of the knowledge of good and evil. God also made woman, a help for Adam, and named her Eve.

Along with the instruction not to eat of the tree of knowledge of good and evil came a warning, 'in the day you eat of it' you *"will surely die."* (Genesis 2:17). Adam and Eve <u>did</u> eat of the fruit of the tree and were immediately aware of their sin. They sewed together leaves to cover their nakedness. Then they hid from God in shame. Part of the curse that came upon Adam and Eve and all of their descendants that day was physical death. Another part of the curse was that they were banished from the Garden of Eden. The intimate fellowship they had enjoyed with God ended. Romans 5:12 says *"Wherefore, as by one man sin entered into the world, and death by sin; and so death passed unto all men, for that all have sinned."* Our parents, Adam and Eve, passed the curse of sin down to every one of us.[20]

These two curses, physical death and separation from God, have followed mankind since that day in the Garden. However, God, in His infinite grace, made a way for the curse to turn to a blessing. *"For God so loved the world, that he gave his only begotten Son, that whosoever believeth in him should not perish, but have everlasting life."* (John 3:16).

There are a few simple steps to become a saint, a child of God. They are simple to follow but hard for the proud sinner to do.

◊ First, recognize that you are a sinner.
- *"For all have sinned, and come short of the glory of God." (Romans 3:23.) God leaves no room for doubt. We ALL have sinned and we ALL fall short of the glory of God.*
- *"As it is written, "There is none righteous, no, not one."" (Romans 3:10.) Again it is plainly stated, none of us have a righteousness of our own to commend us to God – not Billy Graham, not Mother Theresa, not you, not me.*

---

20 Except for Jesus who was born of a virgin and had no earthly father.

◊ Realize that there is a penalty for sin.
- *"For the wages of sin is death" (Romans 6:23a). Just as death followed Adam and Eve's sin so it follows ours. And just as part of the curse for Adam and Eve was separation from God, so it is for you and me as well.*

◊ Believe that God provided a payment of the penalty for your sin.
- *"But God commendeth his love toward us, in that, while we were yet sinners, Christ died for us." (Romans 5:8)*
- *"But the gift of God is eternal life, through Jesus Christ our Lord." (Romans 6:23b). This is a gift from God. It is not something we earn by our good works outweighing our sins.*
- *"For by grace are ye saved, through faith; and not that of yourselves: it is the gift of God: not of works, lest any man should boast." (Ephesians 2:8-9).*

◊ Understand that we have to accept the gift. It is not automatically given because we are good enough, nor does God force us to take the gift. We must accept it, asking Him to forgive us for our sins.
- *"For whosoever shall call upon the name of the Lord shall be saved." (Romans 10:13)*
- *"That if thou shalt confess with thy mouth the Lord Jesus, and shalt believe in thine heart that God hath raised him from the dead, thou shalt be saved. For with the heart man believeth unto righteousness; and with the mouth confession is made unto salvation." (Romans 10:9-10).*

God says that if we honestly follow the steps above that He will save us and we will be one of His saints.

It is not a church, it is not a denomination, nor is it being raised in a good family that saves us. *"Therefore being justified by faith, we have peace with God through our Lord Jesus Christ: By whom also we have access by faith into this grace wherein we stand, and rejoice in hope of the glory of God."* (Romans 5:1-2)

He says once we are one of His saints there is no fear of condemnation. *"There is therefore now no condemnation to them which are in Christ Jesus, who walk not after the flesh, but after the Spirit."* (Romans 8:1)

He says that there is nothing that can separate His saints from Himself. *"For I am persuaded, that neither death, nor life, nor angels, nor principalities, nor powers, nor things present, nor things to come, nor height, nor depth, nor any other creature, shall be able to separate us from the love of God, which is in Christ Jesus our Lord."* (Romans 8:38-39)

Did you notice that there is NOTHING that can separate us from Him? The very first thing mentioned that cannot separate us from God is death! If we are one of His saints, our death will be precious in His sight. He will come to walk through the valley of the shadow of death with us—just as He did for Moses and for Stephen.

Heaven -Or- Hell

There are many who believe that all will go to heaven. We have been told that hell is a teaching left over from the old days. Many are too 'enlightened' now to believe what the Bible clearly teaches. They believe that God could not be a loving God and send anyone to hell.

The book of Revelation says that nothing will enter the new heaven that will defile it. This includes sinners who are not made clean by the work of Jesus Christ on Calvary. Only the ones whose names are written in the Lamb's book of Life will enter this land. *"And there shall in no wise enter into it any thing that defileth, neither whatsoever worketh abomination, or maketh a lie: but they which are written in the Lamb's book of life."* (Revelation 21:27).

Some believe in hell, but believe it is reserved for people who did not do enough good works. It is common for people to say "I am sure that my good works will outweigh my bad." God sent His Son to live on this earth as a pattern for our life. Jesus was crucified on a cross to die for our sins. God requires payment for sin, and only the perfect Son of God could make that payment. There are only two options left for us: accept Christ or reject Him.

In the book of Genesis, God says that Adam's and Eve's sin brought upon them, and then unto us, the curse of death. We have been living under this curse since that time. Unfortunately, some choose to live throughout eternity under that curse. For those who reject the work of Christ on the cross, the book of Revelation describes their judgment *"And I saw a great white throne, and him that sat on it, from whose face the earth and the heaven fled away; and there was found no place for them. And I saw the dead, small and great, stand before God; and the books were opened: and another book was opened, which is the book of life: and the dead were judged out of those things which were written in the books, according to their works. And the sea gave up the dead which were in it; and death and hell delivered up the dead which were in them: and they were judged every man according to their works. And death and hell were cast into the lake of fire. This is the second death. And whosoever was not found written in the book of life was cast into the lake of fire."* (Revelation 20:11-15). Only the names of the saints are written in the Book of Life.

God will someday wipe away all tears and abolish death for His saints, *"And I heard a great voice out of heaven saying, Behold, the tabernacle of God is with men, and he will dwell with them, and they shall be his people, and God himself shall be with them, and be their God. And God shall wipe away all tears from their eyes; and there shall be no more death, neither sorrow, nor crying, neither shall there be any more pain: for the former things are passed away. And he that sat upon the throne said, Behold, I make all things new. And he said unto me, Write: for these words are true and faithful."* (Revelation 21:3-5).

Revelation 22:3 says there will *"be no more curse."* The curse that came upon man in the book of Genesis will be done away with. The curse of death will be done away with. The curse of separation from God will be erased, as the saints spend all of eternity with Him.

God will make all things new. He will abolish death, sorrow, crying, and pain. The beautiful Garden of Eden, inhabited by the very presence of God, was a foreshadow of what was to come. But heaven is reserved only for the saints of God.

When we get to this point in the Biblical record there are no more chances to accept Christ's work, there is no more time to confess your need of a Savior, there is no more time to choose heaven over hell. *"He that is unjust, let him be unjust still: and he which is filthy, let him be filthy still: and he that is righteous, let him be righteous still: and he that is holy, let him be holy still"* (Revelation 22:11). The unsaved will be unsaved forever and the saints will be saints forever.

It is up to you to decide whether to choose heaven with God or hell with the Devil and his demons. I hope and pray that you choose Jesus Christ. You can choose Him right now, before it is too late.

The next step is to find a good church where you can grow in your faith. This is something that you need to pray about, seeking the Lord's wisdom in helping you make that important decision.

Salvation

If you would like to accept Jesus Christ as your personal Saviour so you can be sure that you will go to heaven when you die, you can pray the following prayer.

God I know that I am a sinner based on your word that I have just read. God I understand that you sent your only Son Jesus Christ to die upon that cross and shed His blood for my sins. I am sorry for my sins and with my whole heart I accept Jesus Christ as my Saviour. I believe that He died, rose from the grave and is alive today. I desire for You to take over my life and I will serve You forever. Thank You Jesus for saving me.

Signed_____

It is not the prayer that saves you, it is the work of Jesus Christ on the cross of Calvary that pays the entire penalty for you sin.

If you pray this prayer, please contact me and share the good news. We will rejoice together.

Karl Crawford: karl@pinetreeministries.org

Or you may use the address in the front of this book to send me a letter of what Jesus has done in your heart.

www.ingramcontent.com/pod-product-compliance
Lightning Source LLC
Chambersburg PA
CBHW060605030426
42337CB00019B/3612